FOOD TRUCK GUIDE

How To Start

I0490391

Develop

And

Maintain

A Successful Food Truck Business

LOUISE EVANS

TABLE OF CONTENT

CHAPTER ONE

INTRODUCTION

RESEARCH AND PLANNING

MARKET RESEARCH

FINANCIAL PLANNING

CHAPTER TWO

BUILDING YOUR BRAND

CHAPTER THREE

OPERATING AND GROWING YOUR FOOD TRUCK BUSINESS

FINDING AND BOOKING EVENT

. FOOD SAFETY AND SANITATION

CHAPTER ONE

INTRODUCTION

Starting a food trucking business can be an exciting and profitable venture. A food truck business offers the flexibility to go to where the customers are and the opportunity to serve up delicious meals to hungry customers. Plus, it's a great way to get creative in the kitchen and create unique dishes that will wow your customers. Starting a food truck business requires careful planning, research, and a passion for food. You'll need to obtain permits and licenses, rent or buy a truck, find a location to serve food, and create a menu that will make people come back for more. With the right strategy and dedication, you can create a successful food truck business

RESEARCH AND PLANNING

RESEARCH

Starting a food trucking business requires a great deal of research and planning. Before launching a business, it is important to understand the local regulations and laws that govern the industry. Additionally, it is important to research the local market and potential competitors. Additionally, research should be conducted into the types of food trucks available and the associated costs. Further, the type of equipment needed to operate a food truck must be researched and purchased. This includes refrigerators, food processors, grills, and other items.

Beyond the equipment, research should also be conducted into the types of food to be served. This includes researching popular foods in the area and the cost of ingredients. Additionally, research should be conducted into potential suppliers of ingredients and equipment.
Finally, research should be conducted into the best places to park a food truck. This includes areas with high foot traffic, such as near universities, parks, and other public areas. Additionally,

research should be conducted into the cost of renting parking spaces, as well as any associated taxes and fees.

Overall, starting a food trucking business requires a great deal of research and planning. It is important to thoroughly understand the local regulations, the local market, and potential competitors. Additionally, research should be conducted into the type of equipment, food, and suppliers needed to operate the business. Finally, research should be conducted into the best places to park the food truck. By conducting thorough research and planning, entrepreneurs can ensure that their food trucking business is successful.

PLANNING

1. Research the local regulations: Depending on the state, city, and county you plan to do business in, there may be different regulations in place for operating a food truck. Research what licensing and permits you need in order to legally start a food truck business in your area.

- ☐ Obtain a Business License: Depending on the state or city, you may need to obtain a business license to operate a food truck. Contact your local government to determine the necessary requirements.
- ☐ Acquire Permits: Depending on the county or city, you may be required to obtain a mobile vending permit or a temporary event permit. Additionally, you may need a health permit or a food service permit to operate your truck.

- ☐ Comply with Local Regulations: Depending on the area, there may be certain regulations that must be followed in order to legally operate a food truck. This could include parking regulations, noise ordinances, and any other local restrictions.

- Inspections: Depending on the jurisdiction, you may be required to pass a health inspection in order to gain approval to operate your food truck.

- Insurance: You will likely need to obtain business insurance in order to operate a food truck. This could include general liability, product liability, and property insurance.

- Tax Requirements: You may need to obtain a sales tax permit from your state or local government, as well as collect and pay any applicable taxes.

- **2. Develop a business plan:** Once you have researched what licensing and permits you need, you can start to develop a business plan. This should include information about your target market, the types of food you plan to serve, your pricing strategy, and your marketing plan.

A business plan is an essential tool when starting a food trucking business. It is a document that outlines the goals of the business, how it will be achieved, and the resources needed to make it happen. The plan should include a mission statement, market analysis, competitive analysis, operations plan, financial plan, and a strategy for growth.

The mission statement should be a clear and concise description of the business. It should explain the purpose and values of the business and how it will serve customers.
The market analysis should identify the target market, analyze the competition, and outline strategies for gaining customers. It should also include information on the local and national food truck industry, trends, and customer preferences.

The competitive analysis should compare the business to its competitors. It should include information on pricing, quality of food, customer service, and other factors that differentiate the business from its competitors.

The operations plan should describe the day-to-day operations of the business, such as how food will be prepared, how orders will be taken, and how orders will be delivered. It should include a timeline for launching the business and any necessary permits or licenses.

The financial plan should include a budget, projected income and expenses, and a plan for financing the business. It should also include information on any loans or investments that may be needed to start the business.

The strategy for growth should include plans for expanding the business, such as adding new locations, expanding the menu, or offering catering services. It should also include plans for marketing and advertising the business.

A business plan is an important document that can help guide the success of a food trucking business. It should be updated as the business grows and evolves. By taking the time to develop a business plan, entrepreneurs can ensure that their business is well-positioned for success.

3. Find a food truck: You need to find a truck that meets the local regulations and is suitable for your business. It should have the necessary equipment to prepare and serve food, and enough storage space for supplies.
Starting a food truck company can be a fun and lucrative venture. It is important to do your research to ensure that you choose the right food truck for your business. There are many

factors to consider when selecting the right food truck, such as the size, layout, and features of the truck.

The first step in finding the right food truck is to determine the size of the truck that you need. Depending on the type of food that you plan to serve, the size of the truck can vary significantly. For example, if you plan to serve tacos, a smaller truck may be adequate, while a larger truck may be necessary if you plan to serve burgers.

Next, consider the layout of the truck. The layout of the truck should be determined by the type of food that you plan to serve. For instance, a taco truck may require a more open layout that allows for easy access to the food preparation area, while a more enclosed layout may be better for a burger truck.

Finally, consider the features of the truck. Make sure that the truck has all the features that you need to run your business, such as refrigeration, grills, and other kitchen appliances. Additionally, make sure that the truck meets all applicable health and safety regulations.

Once you have determined the size, layout, and features of the truck that you need, it is time to start looking for a food truck to purchase. Look for used food trucks that are in good condition. You can find used food trucks for sale online, in classifieds, and at auctions. Additionally, consider talking to local food truck owners to see if they have any used trucks that they may be willing to sell.

With the right research and planning, you can easily find a food truck that meets your needs and budget.

4. Create a menu: Create a menu that is unique and appealing to your customers. Consider the type of food you plan to serve, the portion sizes, and the prices.

- ☐ Decide Your Concept: Before you start creating your menu, it's important to decide what type of food you will be serving. Consider the current trends in food, what type of cuisine you plan on offering and what sets you apart from other food trucks.

- ☐ Create a List of Items: Once you have narrowed down your concept, create a list of all the items you plan to serve. This can include sandwiches, tacos, salads, desserts and more. Be sure to include all of the ingredients and flavors you plan to include.

- Price Your Items: After you have created your list of items, it's time to price them. Research the cost of ingredients and labor to determine how much you should charge for each item. Make sure to include a markup for profits.

- Create an Eye-catching Menu: To draw in customers, you need to create an eye-catching menu. You can do this by using bright colors, bold fonts and attractive photographs. This will help to showcase your food and make it more appealing.

- Test Your Menu: Before you launch your food truck, it's important to test your menu. Have friends, family members and colleagues taste your food and give feedback. This helps potential problems to be identified and gives room for adjustments where necessary.

- Promote Your Menu: Once your menu is finalized, you need to promote it. Create flyers and post them around town. Use social media to post pictures of your food and share your menu. You can also offer discounts and specials to attract more customers.

5. Get the necessary permits: Once you have your business plan and menu, you can apply for the necessary permits and licenses. You may need to register with the health department or get a food vendor license.

Obtaining the necessary permits and licenses for starting a food truck business can vary depending on the state and city you are located in. Depending on the size of your business and the type of food you will be serving, you may also need to obtain a food handler's permit or a food service license. Additionally, if you plan to operate on public property or streets, you may need to obtain a permit from the local government.

You may also need to obtain a mobile food vending permit in order to operate in certain areas. This permit will allow you to operate on certain public property or streets, depending on the restrictions in your area. Additionally, you may need to register your business with the state and obtain a seller's permit. Finally, you may need to obtain a commercial vehicle license if you plan to transport food in a vehicle.

It is important to research the specific requirements for your area in order to ensure that you are compliant with all local laws and regulations. Additionally, you should contact your local health department to make sure you are aware of any food safety regulations you must follow in your area.

6. Get the word out: Now that you are ready to launch your business, you need to start marketing your food truck. To promote your business, you can use flyers, social media, and word of mouth.

Create a website or social media page. Having a website or page dedicated to your food truck business is a great way to get the word out. Use it to showcase your menu, post updates and photos, and provide contact information.

- Utilize local resources. Join local food truck associations, attend networking events, and take advantage of local press and media opportunities, such as radio and TV interviews.

- Connect with nearby businesses. Partner with local businesses to host food truck events, advertise on their websites, and offer discounts to their customers.

- Try guerrilla marketing. Take your food truck to busy areas and hand out samples or coupons to draw attention.

- Run promotions. Offer discounts, giveaways, and special offers to attract new customers.

- Leverage word-of-mouth marketing. Ask your satisfied customers to share their experiences with others and leave reviews on your website or social media pages.

- Advertise. Place ads in local publications and on radio, television, and other media outlets.

- Participate in events. Attend local festivals, fairs, and other events to introduce your food truck to potential customers

- Monitor your finances: Keep track of your expenses and income to ensure your business is profitable. Make sure to save some of your profits for future investments and unexpected expenses.

- Develop relationships with customers: Building relationships with customers is essential for a successful food truck business. To keep customers coming back, offer discounts, promotions, and loyalty programs.
- Evaluate and adjust: Once you have been in business for a while, evaluate your performance, make adjustments to your menu and pricing, and determine how you can continue to improve.

7. Purchase or Lease the Right Equipment: Invest in quality equipment that meets the needs of your business. This includes a truck, refrigerator, cooking equipment, and other necessary items.
Purchasing or leasing equipment for a food trucking business can be a big investment, so it's important to carefully weigh the pros and cons of each option before making a decision.

Purchasing equipment may be the best option for some entrepreneurs. It allows them to customize their equipment to fit their specific business needs, and it can be a great way to build equity in their business. It also allows them to have more control over the maintenance and upkeep of their equipment. The downside of purchasing equipment is that it can be costly upfront, and it may also require additional financing or a loan.

Leasing equipment can be a more budget-friendly option for some businesses. It allows entrepreneurs to keep their upfront costs low, and they may even be able to take advantage of tax incentives. Additionally, leasing can make it easier to upgrade equipment as their business grows. However, leasing can also be more expensive in the long run, and it may also require additional paperwork and contracts.

Ultimately, the decision to purchase or lease equipment for a food trucking business should be based on the individual business's needs and goals. Before making a commitment, it is essential to carefully consider all of the factors involved.

MARKET RESEARCH

Starting a food trucking business is a great way to get into the food industry with relatively low start-up costs. However, it's essential to do your market research before committing to this business venture.

First, you need to assess the current market demand for food trucks in your area. Have a look at the competition and research what types of food are in demand. You should also investigate local regulations regarding food trucking, as some cities and states may have different rules and regulations.

Next, you should identify your target customer base. Consider the types of food and beverages you will be selling, as well as the demographic of people who are likely to purchase it. This will help you determine the best locations for your food truck and how to market your business to potential customers.

You should also research the cost of running a food trucking business. This includes things like vehicle insurance, licensing fees, fuel costs, and any other expenses you may incur. Make sure you have an accurate estimate of your fixed and variable costs before investing in a food truck. Finally, you should conduct market research to gauge customer sentiment and feedback. With the help of surveys or focus groups, you can find out what customers think of your food, prices, and
overall customer service. This will help you make changes and improvements to your business and help you to stay competitive in the food trucking market.

By taking the time to do your market research, you will be better prepared to start and maintain a successful food trucking business

FINANCIAL PLANNING

Starting a food truck business can be an incredibly rewarding and profitable endeavor, but it takes careful financial planning to make it successful. Before you begin, you must create a detailed budget for your business. This budget should include the cost of the truck, equipment, supplies, and any necessary permits or licenses. You should also consider the cost of marketing and advertising, insurance, and staffing expenses.
Once you have created a budget, you need to determine how to finance your food truck. You may be able to use your own savings and investments, or you may need to take out a loan. If you choose to take out a loan, you should compare lenders and terms to find the best option for you.

You will also need to consider the potential profits of your food truck, as well as the risks associated with the industry.

Once you have secured financing, you should create a plan to manage your finances. You should track your daily expenses and sales, and create a system to manage cash flow. This will help you stay organized and make sure you are staying within your budget.

Finally, you should consider the long-term financial goals of your food truck business. This could include expanding to multiple locations, investing in additional equipment, or offering catering services. You should create a plan to reach these goals and set milestones to track your progress.

By taking the time to create a detailed financial plan for your food truck business, you can ensure that your business is profitable and successful.

CHAPTER TWO

BUILDING YOUR BRAND

Building a successful brand for a food truck business is a great way to differentiate your product and service from the competition. In a crowded market, having a strong brand can help you stand out and gain new customers. Here are some tips for building a successful brand for your food truck business.

1. Develop a Unique Brand Positioning: Create a unique brand positioning that sets you apart from the competition. Think about the features and benefits that make your food truck business different from others. What makes you stand out? What is the story behind your food truck?

Developing a unique brand position for a food truck business is essential for success. A strong brand position allows customers to identify your business quickly and easily and helps to differentiate you from competitors. Here are some tips for developing a unique brand position for your food truck business:

- Establish a signature dish: Establishing a signature dish is a great way to create a unique brand position. It will help you stand out from the competition and give customers a reason to come to your food truck.

- Create a catchy name: A catchy name can help customers remember your business and make it more memorable. Make sure the name reflects the type of food you serve and is easy to pronounce.

- Develop a unique menu: Developing a menu that is unique and reflects your brand is important. This will help customers recognize your food truck and make it stand out from the competition.

- ☐ Develop a unique style: Developing a unique style for your food truck is essential. This can be done through the design of the truck, the colors, the décor and even the music played.

- ☐ Focus on customer service: Providing excellent customer service is essential for creating a strong brand position. Make sure your food truck staff is friendly and helpful, and that customers are served quickly and efficiently.

2. Create a Logo and Brand Tagline: A great logo and tagline can help establish a strong brand identity. Use your logo and tagline to communicate your brand message and create an emotional connection with your customers.

Creating a logo and brand tagline for starting a food trucking business can be a fun and exciting process! The logo should be visually appealing, memorable and represent the spirit of the food trucking business. The tagline should be concise, catchy and memorable.

When creating a logo, think about what colors and imagery best represent the food trucking business. Consider a bright, bold color palette that reflects the energy and vibrancy of the business. If the food trucking business specializes in a certain type of cuisine, think about incorporating elements of that cuisine into the logo. For example, if the business specializes in Mexican cuisine, consider including imagery of tacos, hot sauce, or cacti.

When creating a tagline, make sure it is concise and memorable. Consider using a pun or a phrase that captures the spirit of the business. This tagline should help customers remember the

food trucking business and what it stands for. For example, a business specializing in Mexican cuisine may have the tagline "Taco 'bout Delicious" or "Taco Tuesday Any Day".

Creating a logo and tagline for a food trucking business can be a fun and rewarding experience. When deciding on the logo and tagline, make sure they reflect the spirit and energy of the business and are memorable. This will help customers remember the business and what it stands for.

3. Develop a Brand Story: Create a compelling brand story that resonates with your target audience. Tell a story that explains why your food truck business exists and what makes it unique.

Starting a food trucking business is an exciting and rewarding adventure. It requires a lot of hard work, dedication, and planning to make it successful. Developing a brand story is an essential part of this process, as it helps define the business and its purpose.

A good brand story starts with understanding the business's values and mission. This can be done by asking yourself questions like: What makes my food truck unique? What kind of food am I selling? What kind of atmosphere will I create? What kind of customer experience am I trying to provide?

Once you have an understanding of the business's values and mission, you can begin to craft the story. Start by introducing the food truck, its concept and any unique features that it offers. For example, if you offer organic and locally-sourced ingredients, make sure to mention this.

Next, explain why the food truck is different than the competition. This can include the quality of food, the customer service, the atmosphere, or any other factors that set it apart. Make sure to emphasize the values and mission of the business in this section.

Finally, provide a call to action. This can be a special offer, a request to follow the food truck on social media, or any other incentive that encourages customers to visit.

By developing a brand story for your food trucking business, you can create an identity and purpose that will draw customers in. It can also help set your business apart from the competition, and ensure that you are providing an experience that customers will enjoy.

4. Strengthen Your Online Presence: Use social media and other digital channels to create a presence online and engage with your customers. Respond to customer reviews, create content that shares your brand message, and use social media to promote your food truck business

Starting a food truck business is an exciting venture that can provide a great opportunity to bring your culinary dreams to life. However, before you can launch your business and start serving up delicious fare to the masses, you need to ensure that your online presence is as strong as possible. Here are some tips for strengthening your online presence when starting a food truck business:

- ☐ Create a Website: A website is an essential part of any business and a great way to showcase your food truck and the food you offer. Make sure that your website is visually appealing, easy to navigate, and regularly updated with new menu items and any special offers or discounts.

- ☐ Develop a Social Media Strategy: Social media is a powerful tool for connecting with potential customers and promoting your business. Establish a presence on one or more of the major social media platforms and create a strategy for how you will use them to engage with your audience. Use popular social media channels like Facebook, Twitter, Instagram, and YouTube to promote your food truck business. Create engaging content that showcases your food, shares your story, and encourages people to patronize your business. Utilize hashtags to reach your target audience and use paid promotions to increase visibility.

- ☐ Utilize Search Engine Optimization (SEO): Using SEO will help your website get found by customers who are searching online for food truck businesses in your area. Include relevant keywords and phrases in your website content and use them naturally throughout your website.

- Leverage Online Reviews: Ask your loyal customers to leave reviews of your food truck on popular review websites such as Yelp and Google. Positive reviews can help attract more customers and boost your online presence.

-

By following these tips, you can ensure that your food truck business has a strong online presence before you launch. Doing so will help you get the word out about your business and make it easier for customers to find and enjoy your delicious fare.

5. Leverage Events and Experiences: Events and experiences are a great way to build your brand and attract new customers. Attend events related to your industry and create unique experiences at your food truck to create a memorable impression. Leveraging events and experiences can be a great way to get your business off the ground.

The first step to leveraging events and experiences is to identify the type of food truck business you want to open. Once you have a plan in place, you can start to look for events and experiences that will give you an opportunity to showcase your food truck. Food festivals, local markets, sporting events, and music festivals are all great places to start.

At these events, you can serve samples of your food, demonstrate your cooking techniques, and create an atmosphere that encourages people to sample your food.

It's also important to make sure you have the right permits and licenses to operate your food truck at these events.

You can also leverage events and experiences to build your brand and create awareness for your food truck. Social media is a great tool to use to promote your food truck and let people know when and where your food truck will be. You can also use events to create an online presence. Creating a website and a blog can help you build a loyal following of customers and give you an opportunity to showcase your food truck and its offerings.

Finally, you can use events and experiences to network with other food truck owners and industry professionals. Networking can help you build relationships, learn from other food truck owners, and gain valuable advice to help you grow your business.

Leveraging events and experiences can be a great way to get your food truck business off the ground. Whether you are looking to gain customers or build your brand, these events can provide you with great opportunities to do both. With the right strategy, you can use these events to create a successful food truck business.

By following these tips, you can create a strong brand for your food truck business that will help differentiate your product and service from the competition. Investing in branding and marketing can help you attract new customers and build a successful business.

6. Local Partnerships: Establish relationships with local businesses and organizations to increase exposure. Offer discounts to their customers and team up with them for joint promotions.

7. Loyalty Programs: Develop a loyalty program to reward customers for their support. This could be anything from small discounts to free meals.

8. Traditional Advertising: Place ads in newspapers, magazines, and on the radio and television. This may be an expensive option, but it can be effective for reaching larger audience.

CHAPTER THREE

OPERATING AND GROWING YOUR FOOD TRUCK BUSINESS

FINDING AND BOOKING EVENTS

Finding and booking events for a food trucking business can be a challenging yet rewarding task. The first step is to decide which type of events you would like to attend. This could include festivals, fairs, corporate events, or even private parties.

Once you have identified the types of events that you would like to attend, the next step is to research and find events that fit your needs.

You can search for events online, in local newspapers, or through event listing services such as Eventbrite. It may also be helpful to reach out to other food truckers in your area to see which events they have attended or plan to attend in the future.

After finding the events that you would like to attend, the next step is to book them. This may involve submitting an application or proposal to the event organizer, as well as paying any necessary fees. Additionally, you will need to make sure that your food truck meets the requirements and regulations of the particular event.

Finally, once you have booked an event, it is important to prepare before the day of the event. This includes making sure that all of your supplies are stocked and ready, as well as making sure
that your food truck is in good working condition. Taking the time to properly prepare for events can help ensure that you have a successful experience.

FOOD SAFETY AND SANITATION

Food safety and sanitation is an essential consideration when starting a food trucking business. Establishing and following health and safety protocols will help protect the health of your customers and ensure the long-term success of your business. After all, if you're going to be serving food to customers, it's essential that it is safe to eat. The following are some essential tips to keep in mind when it comes to food safety while running a food truck business:

The first step to ensuring food safety and sanitation is to obtain a food service license. You will need to check with your local health department to find out what kind of license you need. You may also need to obtain additional permits from your state or local government.

Once your food service license is obtained, you should create a food safety plan that outlines how you will handle food preparation, storage, and service. The plan should address topics such as food storage and temperature control, employee hygiene, and cross-contamination prevention.

You should also establish a system of cleaning and sanitizing all food preparation surfaces, utensils, and equipment. This should be done regularly and thoroughly to prevent the spread of germs and food-borne illnesses.

• **Develop a food safety plan:** Developing a food safety plan is a great way to ensure the safety of the food served at your food truck. This plan should include detailed processes for purchasing, storing, preparing, cooking, and serving food.
• **Follow food safety laws:** Each state has its own food safety laws, so it's important to familiarize yourself with the regulations in your area. This includes keeping up to date with changes in the laws and making sure that your food truck operations comply with them.

• **Train staff:** All of your staff should be trained in food safety and hygiene. This should include topics such as food storage, temperature control, hand washing, using gloves and face masks, and

cross-contamination. Make sure your staff is aware of all local and state food safety requirements, and ensure they understand the importance of following these protocol.

• **Purchase food from reputable sources:** When it comes to the food you serve, you should always purchase your ingredients from reputable sources. This means buying from suppliers who have a good reputation for supplying high-quality ingredients.

• **Ensure food is cooked correctly and stored correctly:** Make sure that all of the food you serve is cooked correctly and stored correctly. This includes ensuring that the food is cooked to the correct temperature and stored at the correct temperature.

• **Clean and sanitize regularly:** Cleaning and sanitizing your food truck regularly is essential for ensuring the safety of the food you serve. This includes washing your hands and all surfaces often, as well as cleaning and sanitizing all of your equipment.

By following these tips, you can ensure that the food served at your food truck business is safe to eat. Food safety should always be a top priority, so make sure that you take the necessary steps to ensure the safety of your customers.

www.ingramcontent.com/pod-product-compliance
Lightning Source LLC
Chambersburg PA
CBHW070319240526
45467CB00046B/2145